In Human Terms

Milet Andrejevic

Balthus

William Beckman

Tibor Csernus

Lucian Freud

John Koch

Michael Leonard

Alfred Leslie

Philip Pearlstein

Sara Rossberg

Library of Congress Catalog Card Number: 91-60964

ISBN: 1-878799-01-0

In Human Terms

Paintings
May 1 – June 1

Works on Paper
June 6 – July 12

1991

Stiebel Modern
32 East 57th Street, New York, New York 10022

Foreword

"In Human Terms" is the inaugural exhibition of Stiebel Modern, the new department of Rosenberg & Stiebel devoted to painterly realism since World War II. Although we received a great deal of support and encouragement as we embarked on this venture, we also heard comments such as: "Stick to what you know," "Why do you want to go into twentieth century? " and "I thought you hated modern art."

In the century since the Stiebel family began dealing in art in Frankfurt-am-Main, we have become known for Old Masters and decorative arts, especially those of 18th century France. Over the decades however, we have also handled the works of then contemporary masters like Matisse and Picasso. In 1988 we held our first modern exhibition *Collecting at the Top*. Our purpose was to introduce the Tate Gallery's newly-formed International Council, led by Gilbert de Botton, whose charter members lent major works from their collections to the exhibition. In 1990 we staged the first New York show of the young Anglo-German artist, Sara Rossberg.

During the Rossberg exhibition, a curator of Old Master paintings at a major American museum came through the gallery and, looking at these painterly realist pictures, said, "They continue the Old Master tradition." That evening my wife and I looked at our library at home and found two full shelves of books of twentieth century painting. These represented monographs and exhibition catalogs of artists we liked a great deal. They were not the painters of abstract art whom the art community has designated a "must" for every serious collector or institution, but rather those who work in a style that has been accepted for the past seven hundred years! (This was nothing new to my wife, as much of her thirteen years at the Metropolitan Museum was devoted to curating twentieth century decorative arts which continued the tradition of craftsmanship from centuries past with a modern interpretation.)

We have found that there is a growing body of work that looks back to the art of the past and interprets it in today's terms. We do not see handling this area of the contemporary spectrum as a change in direction, but rather a continuation of our personal interests and those of Rosenberg & Stiebel. Throughout its history the gallery has added new fields to its repertoire and is proud of its policy of showing works of art that meet our criteria of quality, in many fields.

In addition to the artists who are participating in the debut of Stiebel Modern, I want to thank the many friends who have lent works of art as well as those who have offered us advice and support in the preparation of this exhibition. They include Richard Bellamy, Gilbert de Botton, Jeffrey Deitch, Frank Deldeo, Karen Demuth, Stuart Feld, Jill George, Jill Goodman, Janet Green, James Kirkman, Jan Krugier, Jacqueline Leland, Carole Pesner, the Schoelkopf family, and Michel Soskine.

Gerald G. Stiebel
February, 1991

In Human Terms: An Appreciation

Penelope Hunter-Stiebel

"How can you possibly tell if a contemporary work of art is good? Will it stand the test of time?"

The question was constantly put to me at the Metropolitan Museum of Art when I was acquiring works for the permanent collection of twentieth century decorative arts. In that field there was an academic canon of acceptability based on the International Style of architecture and industrial design. It was brilliantly documented by the Museum of Modern Art and there was no reason to duplicate that collection. Moreover, looking around me I found work that was more meaningful in the context of the Metropolitan's encyclopedic holdings. It was then the 1970s, and the Studio Craft Movement was in full bloom with artists rediscovering traditional disciplines of glassmaking, ceramics, metalwork and textile. Soon I was being asked by curators in other museums for lists of artists whose work I had acquired to reference in building their collections. I wanted to avoid a codified "Met list" but was delighted to introduce colleagues to a different way of looking at the contemporary field.

I did not believe then, and I do not now, that it is necessary to turn one's back on the past in order to advance. One of the curators I most admired at the Metropolitan was Henry Geldzahler. For all his close association with the New York School, this flamboyant figure of the avant-garde could equally appreciate the quality of an 18th century porcelain and defend the virtues of a traditional landscape by a young unknown Rackstraw Downes. For myself I found an aesthetic stumbling block in the generally accepted masterpieces of Abstract Expressionism, so I simply steered clear of contemporary painting during my museum career.

No longer a curator, I can now indulge myself in the pure pleasure of modern paintings that move me. These are works that do not break with history in defiant gestures of alienation, but seek to communicate in human terms using demanding techniques that have been developed over centuries. They are not pitched to critics or the "art public." Theirs is not a raucous fanfare geared to grab attention, but rather a steady pulse, connecting past with future.

The works in this exhibition all address you, and me, individually and collectively, in the most direct visual language. Each is the work of an artist who goes through the crafting of recognizable form to reach beyond it. The shape of the human body as we have seen it and felt it is placed before us, and as we perceive the image we are touched in ways that are difficult to describe.

Why does the little girl looking out from the Balthus canvas cling in memory? The subject of the 1954 painting *Colette assise* was the daughter of a stonemason working on the restoration of the artist's country home, the Château de Chassy. She did not long hold the artist's attention, and was soon replaced by more yielding adolescents in related poses. (The eldest of the *Three Sisters* reclines on a settee in repeated depictions from 1954, and 17 year-old Frédérique, who was to become the favorite model, appears in *The Dream* of 1955 sprawling on the same settee that Colette occupied so demurely).

Balthus painted Colette on one other occasion also in 1954 in a half-length profile. In both depictions the impression of complete normalcy is soon overtaken by fascination. In these honeyed images, laboriously built up of layers of pigment mixed in varnish for an archaic effect recalling Roman wall painting, the girl next door becomes a self-possessed siren. In *Colette assise* she fixes and returns our gaze in quiet challenge. In this image Balthus created a haunting icon of the onset of adolescence.

Lucian Freud's *Pregnant Girl* personifies the primeval female. Belly and breasts swollen with new life distend her angular form to fulfill its biological destiny. Between her neck and shoulders Freud has created a field of pure painting as passionate as Cézanne's *Mont St. Victoire*. Although the flesh is built up of swathes of paint, the force of the subject's person defies abstraction. She turns away, refusing the vanity of portraiture. Locked in the grinding physicality of her condition is the beauty and endurance of the human spirit.

With a pastel palette, Milet Andrejevic paints Elysian fields, classicizing reality to an effect much like the 19th century compositions of Puvis de Chavannes. In *The Musician* we first see Apollo serenading his mythological colleagues before recognizing the landscape of New York's Central Park and the normalcy of its weekend denizens. The artist reveals the calm of a bucolic scene at the very center of the most bustling modern metropolis. He reminds us that our world still retains beauty resembling the ideal of centuries past.

The classicism of Philip Pearlstein is of quite another sort recalling the colossal sculptures of antiquity. But Pearlstein's race of giants in human form who push the confines of his canvases are not idealized demigods. They are none other than the neighbors we stand behind on the supermarket line. Stripped of their clothes they seem endowed with superhuman powers, shocking us into awareness of the strength of our humanity. In a striking composition of 1988 the inverted pose of the model and the airplane propped next to her suggest a graceful titan tumbled from the heavens.

Like Degas, Michael Leonard revels in the aesthetic pleasure of the human body in motion. Isolating elements from everyday gesture, he depicts them with the gentle touch of a lover in canvases of glowing intimacy. He creates passages of abstract lyricism in the crook of an elbow, the angle of a thigh or the arch of a back. As the eye travels around a Leonard composition following the outlines of the model's limbs, the most mundane movement becomes balletic adagio.

Heated sensuality radiates from the 1959 *Nude* by John Koch where the allure of female flesh is heightened by lamplight playing across rounded hips and thighs and silvery sheets. As we read the model's gesture, biting into a perfect, ripe fruit, we know her to be a descendant of Eve. The atmosphere is so perfumed with eroticism that, were it not for the details of contemporary furniture, we could think ourselves in the French Rococo bedrooms of Boucher.

Open air and sunlight make Alfred Leslie's 1987 nude all the more astonishing. Like David's *Madame Récamier*, *Casey Key* is at once an ideal beauty and a forceful figure of her time. Her breathtaking limpid relaxation is born of complete self-confidence. Sunbathing naked, with eyes closed, she remains in control, fingertips on coffee cup, cigarette dangling, half listening to a television program. With apple at hand, she, too, may be the daughter of Eve, and the half-eaten pizza and trail of cookies may signal sensual gratification; but she is no mere sex object. Even exposed she is far from vulnerable, as she awaits the ring of the telephone to spring into action, pencil and pad at the ready. Investing his nude with ethos of Women's Liberation, Leslie has painted a woman who commands admiration and respect.

Darkness cradles the nude painted in 1980 by Tibor Csernus and invokes the legacy of Caravaggio and Velázquez. A cold eerie light shapes the contours of flesh and bone. Is she model or mirage? The ruddy hand of a youth behind her dangles over his chairback, hesitant to touch and test. We share his rapture. In this woman caressed into life by Csernus' loaded brush, we see the chiaroscuro tradition reborn.

In *Diana 9* William Beckman has created a totem. He has clad her image in perfect skin of oil pigment impervious to decay, and raised her to the rank of the Byzantine Empress Theodora whose dark-eyed mosaic image has remained vivid and commanding since the 6th century. Diana requires no robe or crown to assert her dominance. Her unadorned person fills a towering field, and demands you to meet the challenge of seeing her in every detailed particular of frontal nudity. Fixed by her stare, you too feel stripped bare and locked into a wrestling match of wills.

Sara Rossberg's *Layers* is composed of three unlikely bedfellows, a black man, a white man, and an adolescent, individualized with the graphic clarity of disparate figures assembled in a Cranach altarpiece. They have nothing to do with each other beyond the blanket they share, yet that element itself, rendered as a churning mass of orange pigment, provides a powerful matrix. Though visually interlocked, the men are isolated each within themselves, the black man reading his newspaper, the pensive white man staring at his hands. The boy's eyes are glazed over in adolescent malaise. He looks as if he would gladly sacrifice self to merge with the orange matrix with which his unruly red hair has already joined. There is neither release nor connection to be had in this metaphor of urban circumstance where proximity does not entail relationship and every man remains an island.

Each viewer brings his own associations to such works, combining and adding them to the artist's impulse. The response is all the more intense for being uniquely personal. Further resonances can be established in an exhibition in a space as intimate as Stiebel Modern. In this circumstance the works can speak not only to the viewer, but to each other. The viewer becomes part of an expanded counterpoint of reverberating associations as each artist's voice rings out distinctly while it enriches the fugue.

"Is it good? Will it last?"

Each work in this exhibition gives its answer directly in human terms.

The Realist's Path

Katherine Chapin

Contemporary realism is based on the human desire to communicate. The realist's decision is to use the visually recognizable as a contact point. Because individuality and the subjectivity of perception are human, too, as Robert Hughes puts it "realism has come back in as many forms as there are painters."[1]

The continuing tradition of representation in its variant forms is the foundation of *In Human Terms*. The exhibition is not only about artists who use the figure as a vehicle for expression, but also about the continuum of the realist style over the past 40 years. Rather than relying on written theory to communicate the work's purpose, these artists have combined their passion for human experience with a high level of academic painting ability. Artists in this exhibition are inspired by their own thoughts, emotions, the broader influence of art history, as well as formal issues, rather than specifically working within the narrower trends of their contemporary art community.

Many artists working in this style have achieved recognition in spite of the fact that they have stayed outside prevailing fashions and related publicity. Through the tides of Surrealism, Dadaism, the New York School, Abstract Expressionism, Pop Art, Photorealism, Neo-Expressionism, then to Post-Modernism and all of its sub-categories, painterly realists have worked separately, and most of the time quietly, in a continuing fascination with the figure and its ability to communicate both human issues and art issues. Though painterly realism has enjoyed acknowledgement at various times under various headings, the artists working in this mode have never really been linked or critically identified as a school. Because every artist's and every viewer's specific idea of reality is subjective, and always changing with the world's environment, realism does not lend itself to definition or categorization.

The 1940s saw the emergence of an avant-garde that was specifically against realistic representation, and artists who maintained the traditional values in painting were challenged for the first time. As Abstract Expressionism became the dominant international art movement, realism came to be seen not only as *retardataire*, but also as a reactionary and unsophisticated art form. However, the ensuing decades proved that this viewpoint would not prevent painters from making the unpopular choice – to paint what they saw and to disregard Modernist doctrines. It has become evident by the quality, sincerity, and unlikely success of some contemporary painters that realism is not necessarily a reaction to the avant garde, but in fact a form that some artists will choose regardless of the time period in which they are working.

There have been moments over the past four decades when Realism has been "re-discovered" or thought of as a "new trend," but these moments never really lasted any longer than other media–generated trends. Most recently, in 1981, Frank Goodyear at the Pennsylvania Academy put together a major exhibition of realist art and the accompanying catalog *Contemporary Realism Since 1960*. In his review, Hilton Kramer wrote "...the realist movement itself – despite the quarrels that afflict it... is not about to diminish or disappear. It has succeeded in reestablishing something fundamental to the art life of our time – a way of thinking about art that binds its forms, its imagery, and the very process of its creation to the act of individual perception, to the self as it negotiates its difficult progress in the world of experience. This was precisely the development that Modernist art ... had long told us was moribund and out of reach, outdated and exhausted. How amazing, then, that it should – against such odds – now be thriving with so much energy and talent! For the moment, it is astonishing that it has won so conspicuous a place in an art world that was hardly prepared to receive it."[2]

The Pennsylvania Academy exhibition, along with a proliferation of other international exhibitions, made the press turn its attention, briefly, to realist painting in the current environment. *Art In America* devoted the entire September 1981 issue to the "New Realism," with many top critics reporting on the new approaches being used by artists such as Pearlstein, Beckman, Beal, Leslie and the Photorealists. However, in 1982, when Neo-Expressionism came to the fore, realists were again considered *retardataire.*

Unlike work produced within critical schools, such as Minimalism, Color Field painting, and Post Modernism, realist painting does not attempt to convey a specific meaning, or "punch line" to be "gotten," and once "gotten" filed away as "understood." Frank Stella said: "I always get into arguments with people who want to retain the old values in painting – the humanistic values that they always find on the canvas. My painting is based on the fact that only what can be seen is there...what you see is what you see."[3] If one were looking at one of Stella's paintings 200 years from now, and did not understand this basic principle, there would be no way of seeing the artist's intention. As there is no human connection with what is "there" – no reference to what is meant to be perceived, the written explanation will have to accompany this type of expression throughout history.

Since the mid 1940s, the focus on issues of abstraction and concept, and rejection of what Stella refers to as "the old values in painting," has made it difficult for students to find instruction in "traditional" painting. Because of this, many realist artists are self-taught. They have developed their painting techniques and compositional concepts through looking at those of the Old Masters. In this way, they have actually opened up a broader spectrum of seeing that includes not just their own contemporary ideas of light, form, and volume, but also the ideas that have withstood the test of time.

Born in Paris in 1908, Balthazar Klossowski de Rola (Balthus) grew up in a very lively, artistic atmosphere. His mother, a painter, and father, a stage designer, were friends of the poet Rainer Maria Rilke, who encouraged the young Balthus to persue his artistic talents. At the age of 16 he decided to devote himself entirely to art. He had received no formal training in painting, other than some live model drawing sessions given by Bonnard and Vlaminck. Instead he found inspiration in the works of Poussin and Piero della Francesca.

For more than 70 years, Balthus has remained committed to his own vision, and has maintained that his use of representation, putting down the way things appeared to him, is focused on the play of structures and their relationships. Though not universally believed by his viewers, Balthus has said that the sexuality of the adolescent girls is not an issue in his painting[4] but that he has used them as volumes to shape space – as formal elements in his own created environment. The paintings are ultimately the artist's vision of reality, brought into two dimensions, and the viewer is allowed to react subjectively to that reality and draw his own conclusions.

Balthus was friendly with the Surrealists and Existentialists, especially Artaud, Paul Eluard, Camus, and Malraux. They admired Balthus because of the unconscious element and dreamlike quality of some of his paintings. Though he could have been influenced by this dogmatic group, Balthus kept his own way. Artaud called the paintings "Organic Realism", and a "reaction against Surrealism," and others grouped him with the Neo–Romantics. Still others attempted to connect his work with the Neue Sachlichkeit (New Objectivity), though his work has no direct relationship with the self-conscious attitude toward realism found in the work of Otto Dix and George Grosz.

Sabine Rewald points out, in her 1984 essay for Balthus' retrospective exhibition catalog, that "Indeed it is by avoiding labels and concentrating on differences between his art and that of his contemporaries that we can best perceive and appreciate Balthus' inimitable qualities."[5]

John Koch was born one year after Balthus, 3,000 miles away in Toledo, Ohio. He also began painting seriously at a very young age, and had very little formal training. At age 14 he was doing portrait commissions during summers in Provincetown, Massachussetts and at 19, like any aspiring artist of the day, he went to study in Paris where he remained until 1922. Upon finishing his own independent program of study in Europe, Koch came back to the United States and settled in New York. He held his first solo exhibition in 1935 and exhibited regularly until his death in 1978.

Koch was virtually untouched by any of his contemporaries' tendencies toward abstraction and conceptualism, and his style was consistent throughout his career. He adopted the Old Master technique of egg tempera with oil glazing, and the influence of Vermeer has been noted in the clarity and serenity of his interior scenes. Although he was exposed to Cubists' and Surrealists' Paris at an impressionable age, and then lived and worked in the midst of the New York art world which was obsessed by the avant garde, Koch continued to paint and exhibit realist works. Mario Amaya, in his essay for the painter's 1973 exhibition at The New York Cultural Center wrote: "A Koch is always a Koch, and dramatic stylistic changes, broken into periods do not, nor, I would predict, will ever exist in his work."[6]

Of his own work, Koch said in 1972: "I am quite visibly a realist, occupied essentially with human beings, the environments they create, and their relationships. In regard to technique, I increasingly tend toward a technique which conceals itself, which does not obtrude upon or attempt to replace the essential human communication."[7] Here is the opposing side of Frank Stella's argument – Koch felt that what you see, in fact, should not be just what you see, but it should be an illusion that opens the door to a human, emotional response.

Lucian Freud, on the other hand, is an artist who believes that what he paints is the objective, true-to-life reality that he sees in his studio, and not an illusion that is designed to manipulate the viewer. Freud, in effect is saying "what you see is what you see," only with the intention of capturing a reality, rather than the properties of paint and canvas, as Stella offers.

Lucian Freud was born in Berlin in 1922, where he lived with his family until 1933, when they were forced to move to London. Having shown a talent for drawing, Freud was enrolled at a school in London run by the self-taught artist Cedric Morris who promoted self-teaching as the route to true expression. Since his debut in London as a boy prodigy, Freud's talent has defied categorization. His early portraits and interiors seemed oddly linear and defined, and did not really fit in with the Neo–Romantics' painterly effects or the nostalgic attitudes of the School of Paris that were in fashion in the 1940s in Europe. At that time, critics attempted to put a label on Freud, despite his individuality, dubbing him "the Ingres of Existentialism."[8] Others pressed him for connections to Surrealism. Though Freud denies this influence, he has admitted admiration for the detachment, solitude, and remoteness achieved by such artists as Miró and de Chirico.

Remoteness has remained a constant in Freud's work, although his painting style and critical labels have changed. When he switched from sable to boar's hair brushes, the crisp, flattened quality of his figures evolved into a textured, layered, and shockingly "real" characters reminiscent of Frans Hals. In the latter phase he has become identified with the "School of London," a disparate group of artists which includes Kitaj, Francis Bacon, and Frank Auerbach. However, Freud has put realism before anything else, and so much so that in 1987 Robert Hughes proclaimed "Lucian Freud has become the greatest living realist painter."[9]

Though Lucian Freud has been recognized in Great Britain since his youth, his work has only come to be known on an international scale relatively recently. He has not yet had a major painting exhibition in New York, though his 1987 travelling retrospective came to Washington D.C., and his work is included in many major museum collections the world over.

Milet Andrejevic, born in 1925, grew up in Yugoslavia and had his first exhibition in Belgrade in 1956. When he moved to New York at the age of 33, he was working with Geometric Abstraction and exhibited with the Green Gallery, whose stable of artists included Mark diSuvero, Lucas Samaras, and George Segal. In the 1960s Andrejevic became a Pop artist, and by the 1970s, his work took a radical turn, and he began painting his personal Arcadian vision – a world that had deep connections to history and nature. Andrejevic brought utopian landscapes, like those of Puvis de Chavannes, together with the contemporary figure, in order to show that the traditions of human behavior are as old as the gods themselves. Of his painting, Hilton Kramer wrote: "His strongest affinities are obviously with painters from an earlier age, and while his subject matter is unquestionably contemporary, his attitude is not ... This is fundamentally Modernist in spirit, and yet never shirks the traditional obligation of realism to give us a persuasive account of the concrete world 'out there.'"[10]

Philip Pearlstein, born in 1924, has always had a fascination with art history as well as painting. His earliest works as a high school student were done in the Ash Can style of Reginald Marsh, but, as he began to develop his understanding of the art world, he became an Abstract Expressionist. When he was 34, he went to Italy on a Fulbright grant and made formal studies of the Roman ruins which he planned to translate into abstract paintings. He became interested in the tension caused by suppressing the romantic sentiment of the ruins, and making them into his own "found objects." He began to pull the energy of the recognizable and bring it into a different, objectified realm.

On his return to New York, Pearlstein continued dealing with the formal problems that he applied in his Abstract Expressionist style, but turned to the nude for content. In his subsequent paintings of the nude-as-object, he continued to strive for the same translation of the subjective to the objective – divesting the nude of its eroticism and personality. By removing these associations, Pearlstein intentionally provokes the viewer.

Pearlstein started working with representation specifically as a reaction to Abstract Expressionism. In 1962, Pearlstein wrote a manifesto of a new figurative realism entitled *Figure Painters Today Art Not Made in Heaven,* and was dubbed "Father of a 'New Realism.'" In a 1981 interview the artist asserted: "Previously, anyone who wanted to be a realist in this century modified their view of nature according to rules of abstraction. They were willing to distort, to make things conform to an abstract scheme. I think the three of us (Pearlstein, Gabriel Laderman and Sam Gelber) reversed the procedure, finding abstraction in nature, rather than making nature correspond to abstraction."[11]

Alfred Leslie, born in 1927 in the Bronx, also belonged to the generation of the Abstract Expressionists. At the age of 16, Leslie studied film-making and painting at the Art Students League and at Pratt in New York. He became interested in pre-war and contemporary European ideas of such artists as Piet Mondrian and Kurt Schwitters, and found a place in the community of the emerging artists of the New York School. When he first started exhibiting in 1951, his paintings and collages of found materials were mainly abstract. In the late 1950s, Leslie began collaborating on films with Frank O'Hara, a poet and curator at the Museum of Modern Art.

While working on films, Leslie continued to paint, slowly moving away from abstraction, toward a more literal narrative content. The paintings of this transitional period, were lost when his studio burned in 1966. Without his studio, he felt he could no longer make films, and incorporated his cinematic ideas into his paintings and drawings. The same year as the fire, Frank O'Hara was killed in an automobile accident, and from 1967 to 1973 Leslie devoted himself to a series of paintings documenting the moments before O'Hara's death. In this series, *The Killing Cycle*, Leslie's figures became dramatic and allegorical, as impending consequence and the intrinsic passion were his subject matter.

In 1969, Leslie became a founding member of the Figuration Alliance, which was organized as a forum for maverick realists. The group, which met at Leslie's loft, was mainly comprised of artists who were interested in working from the live studio model. The formation of the Alliance was a response to Modernism's cold art-about-art doctrine. In Leslie's works the aim was, and is still, to "put back into art all the painting that the Modernists took out by restoring the practice of 20th century painting"[12] and "...to establish immediate contact with the most casual viewers, so as to surprise them, hoping that if they could care for a picture of a person seen so unexpectedly, perhaps some of that care could be transferred into their own lives and their attitudes toward others."[13] This humanistic ideal is still central to the drawings and paintings that come from Leslie's New York studio today.

Also born in 1927, the Hungarian painter Tibor Csernus studied in Budapest under devotees of German Expressionism. Going against the grain of his professors and fellow students, he taught himself about figuration and the Old Master technique by looking at the work of Caravaggio, and Velázquez. Csernus moved to Paris in 1964, where he has remained since.

His first exhibition in the United States was not until 1985. It had been eagerly awaited by the artists who had followed his work from reproductions and visits abroad. After this show, Jack Beal, the renowned realist painter, published a letter to Tibor Csernus in *Art In America*. Beal pointed out the magical balance Csernus had achieved by painting the figure realistically in illusionistic space, and, at the same time, embracing contemporary issues of expressionistic painting: "Strangely, often what is not delineated becomes as clear as that which is crystalline. These deliberate ambiguities invoke a level of visual excitement which can only exist in realist art."[14]

Beal put Csernus' devotion to Caravaggio into historical perspective: "Ribera and Velázquez, Honthorst and TerBruggen, Rembrandt and Rubens, de la Tour and Valentin de Boulogne (and now Tibor Csernus) have displayed an honest admiration and comprehension of the work of the most influential painter (and most positive force) in the history of Art: their humility and willingness to learn led to profound changes in perception and execution–should we ask for less in our own time?"[15]

Michael Leonard's paintings also remind us of the achievements of the Old Masters and sustain a contemporary quality. Born in India in 1933, Leonard moved to London where he studied fine arts and graphic design. After graduation in 1957, Leonard became a free-lance illustrator. On lunch hours spent in London's National Gallery, he "woke up to the formal delight" of great paintings, particularly those of Poussin and Degas. He saw that the key to emotional response lay as much in the organization of a composition as in its content. His first paintings were surrealistic, but he abandoned that approach as he found that there was not enough discipline in dreams: "you can just keep altering the painting forever because there is no logic."[16] He instead found that order of real life provided the rational structure he sought.

By the end of the 1960s, Leonard began to devote more and more time to his own painting, though he felt displaced among the abstractionists and Pop artists who dominated the galleries and art press. In the mid-1970s, he met Lincoln Kirstein, who showed him a catalog of the 1950 exhibition he had organized, titled "Symbolic Realism in American Painting, 1940–1950." Even in reproduction, the work of Paul Cadmus, Peter Blume, George Tooker, and their associates showed Leonard a 20th century context to which he could relate. He came to the realization that the highly-crafted portraits and figures he had been doing in his studio might in fact have a place in the outside world.

This has been confirmed over the past decades, with regular London exhibitions at Fischer Fine Art, a retrospective at the 1989 Festival of Bath, important commissions (including the portrait of Queen Elizabeth for the National Portrait Gallery), and a steady stream of publications, including a monograph with introductions by Lincoln Kirstein and Edward Lucie-Smith.

William Beckman's contact with Old Master paintings, and subsequent career as an artist came practically by accident. Born in 1942 in a tiny Minnesota farming community, he had no contact with the visual arts as an organized entity, until the age of 19, when he moved to Minneapolis. His apartment was across from the Art Institute, and one day he ventured inside to discover paintings by Rembrandt, Corot and Courbet. Beckman said of this experience: "Looking at the individual portraits, I felt as if I were communicating directly with the painters and the subjects communicated with me directly."[17] Beckman's own approach to the figure has everything to do with facing the figure (and the figure facing the viewer) straight on.

The interplay between the viewer and subject has been central to Beckman's work since his graduate studies at the University of Iowa. At that time he was constructing boxes with mirrors and miniature paintings that recall the concerns of 17th century Dutch artists. The boxes dealt with perspective and the issues of our perception of space. What was seemingly direct, was not quite so.

In 1969, Beckman moved to New York, where he had heard that there were other artists working in styles that related to his. By sheer chance he rented Alfred Leslie's loft, where the meetings of the Figuration Alliance were held. Beckman, using the subject matter that was available – himself and his wife – began to paint frontal portraits whose psychological power has grown over the years. He was included in the Philadelphia Academy's *Contemporary Realism Since 1960* exhibition in 1981, and has been in many important exhibitions before and since. According to Carl Belz, "... his images are as substantial and convincing as any in the art of our time, his ambition for figuration virtually unparalleled. His realism, however, is rooted in the Modernist sensibility, in the urge not simply to depict or ideate the world, but to express the problematic relationship to it that attends our self-consciousness within it."[18]

Sara Rossberg was born in 1952 in Recklinghausen, Germany. She has never identified with any group of artists or tried to be part of one. She studied at the Frankfurt Academy of Fine Art and won a prestigious German government grant which entailed study abroad. Her Frankfurt professors emphasized the necessity of doing something "new," but also something that achieved her own individual and personal goal for expression. Using the tightly-painted figure was somewhat radical, compared to the Beuys-trained conceptualists and the Neo-Expressionists around her, but she was encouraged to do what she wanted to do. When the time came to go abroad, she chose London and the Camberwell School of Art, where she found "as long as you painted like Cezanne, you were O.K." She continued her own program of development and after graduating in 1978, she remained in London, where she lives and works.

Like Beckman, what has come to interest her is the psychological aspect of characters and their relationships. Her paintings of interior scenes and the formal precision with which they are built, however, speak of Balthus' concerns. John Russell Taylor has characterized this dichotomy as "Romanticism rigorously controlled by classical discipline."[19]

Edward Lucie-Smith has written that Rossberg "is a humanist painter, and the communication she wants to initiate is communication on a level of direct and simple human feeling. We respect her for the same reason that we respect 16th century Italian portraitists such as Domenico Moroni, for the sense of emotional openness and fullness which she is able to achieve. We respect her further, because we know that such qualities have become very rare in the art of our time."[20]

"In Human Terms" brings together ten artists that possess the rare qualities that Edward Lucie-Smith speaks of. Each artist, whether from Western Europe, Midwestern America, the Eastern Block, or the Bronx, has found his or her own path to the figure. Each has brought forth the issues of humanity that are relevant now and will remain so throughout history. Though the way these paintings are seen may change over the course of time, there will always be the contact point of the human spirit as portrayed by their creators. Regardless of the achievements of Modernist theory, and the innovations of the avant-garde, realism will live on. This continuing tradition is described by Alexander Eliot who wrote of its exponents: "they create not just the appearance of things as they are, but a larger truth that combines the world of visible objects with the invisible world of man's ideas. Informing the purely physical with the human thoughts and feelings, they enhance both worlds."[21]

FOOTNOTES

1. Hughes, Robert. Quotation from Time, November 29, 1976 In John Arthur's, *Spirit of Place: Contemporary Landscape Painting and the American Tradition.* (Boston, Toronto, London: Bulfinch Press, Little Brown and Company, 1989), 65.
2. Kramer, Hilton. Reprint of October 25, 1981 Article in *The Revenge of the Philistines. New* York: The Free Press, 1985),366.
3. Tomkins, Calvin. Reprint of September 1984 Article in *Post- to Neo-: The Art World of The1980s.* (New York: Penguin Books, 1989),163.
4. Rewald, Sabine. *Balthus.* (New York: The Metropolitan Museum of Art, 1984),41.
5. Ibid., 37.
6. Amaya, Mario. *John Koch.* (New York: The New York Cultural Center, 1973),5.
7. Ibid., 6.
8. Gowing, Lawrence. *Lucian Freud.* (New York: Thames and Hudson, 1982),29.
9. Hughes, Robert. *Lucian Freud Paintings.* (New York: Thames and Hudson, 1987),7.
10. Kramer, Hilton. Reprint of January 11, 1981 Article in *The Revenge of the Philistines.* (New York: The Free Press, 1985),244.
11. Shaman, Sanford Sivitz. "An Interview with Philip Pearlstein." *Art in America* (September1981):122.
12. Lucie-Smith, Edward. *Art in the Seventies.* (Ithaca, New York: Cornell University Press,1980),68.
13. Jencks, Charles. *Post-Modernism: The New Classicism in Art and Architecture.* (New York: Rizzoli, 1987),517.
14. Beal, Jack. "A Letter to Tibor Csernus." *Arts Magazine* (May 1985):130-131.
15 Ibid.
16. Interview with Michael Leonard, February 9, 1991.
17 Arthur, John. *Realists at Work.* (New York: Watson-Guptill Publications, Inc., 1983),31
18. Belz, Carl. "A Conditional Paradise." *Art In America* (January 1989):140.
19. Taylor, John Russell. *Sara Rossberg, New Paintings.* (London: Thumb Gallery,1988).
20. Lucie-Smith, Edward. "Sara Rossberg." In *Sara Rossberg Figuratively Speaking.* (New York: Rosenberg & Stiebel, 1990),14.
21. Eliot, Alexander. *Three Hundred Years of American Painting.* (New York: Time, Inc., 1957), 20.

BIBLIOGRAPHY

Adams, Henry. *Thomas Hart Benton; An American Original.* New York: Alfred A. Knopf, 1989.

Alloway, Lawrence. "The Renewal of Realist Criticism." *Art in America* (September 1981):108-111.

Amaya, Mario. *John Koch.* New York: The New York Cultural Center, 1973.

Arthur, John. *Spirit of Place: Contemporary Landscape Painting and the American Tradition.* Boston, Toronto, London: Bulfinch Press, Little Brown & Co., 1989.
——. *Realists at Work.* New York: Watson-Guptill Publications, 1983.
——. *Realist Drawings & Watercolors.* Boston: New York Graphic Society, 1980.

Beal, Jack. "A Letter to Tibor Csernus." *Arts Magazine* (May 1985):130-131.

Belz, Carl. "A Conditional Paradise." *Art In America* (January 1989): 136-141.

Coppet, Laura de and Alan Jones. *The Art Dealers.* New York: Clarkson N. Potter, 1984.

Eliot, Alexander. *Three Hundred Years of American Painting.* New York: Time, Inc., 1957.

Goodyear, Frank H., Jr. *Contemporary American Realism since 1960.* Boston: New York Graphic Society, 1981.

Gowing, Lawrence. *Lucian Freud.* New York: Thames and Hudson, 1982.

Henry, Gerrit. "Painterly Realism and the Modern Landscape." *Art in America* (September 1981):112-121.

Hills, Patricia and Roberta K. Tarbell. *The Figurative Tradition and the Whitney Museum of American Art.* Newark, New Jersey: University of Delaware Press, London and Toronto: Associated University Presses, 1980.

Hughes, Robert. *Lucian Freud Paintings.* New York: Thames and Hudson, 1987.

Jencks, Charles. *Post-Modernism: The New Classicism in Art and Architecture.* New York: Rizzoli, 1987.

Kirsten, Lincoln. *Symbolic Realism in American Painting,*1940-1950. London: The Institute of Contemporary Arts, 1950.

Kramer, Hilton. *The Revenge of the Philistines.* New York: The Free Press, 1985.

Kuspit, Donald B. "What's Real in Realism?" *Art in America* (September 1981):84-95.

Leslie, Alfred, Artist's Statement, March 1, 1991.

Lucie-Smith, Edward. *Art in the Eighties.* New York: Phaidon Universe, 1990.
——. "Sara Rossberg." In *Sara Rossberg Figuratively Speaking.* New York: Rosenberg & Stiebel, Inc., 1990.
——. *Art Now.* Secaucus, New Jersey: The Wellfleet Press, 1989.
——. Foreword to *Michael Leonard, Paintings*, by Lincoln Kirsten. London: GMP, 1985.
. *Art in the Seventies.* Ithaca, New York. Cornell University Press, 1980.

Nochlin, Linda. *Realism.* London: Penguin Books, 1971.
——. "Return to Order." *Art in America* (September 1981):74-83.

Perl, Jed. "Is the New Realism Ready for the Academy?" *Art in America* (September 1981):11-13.

Rewald, Sabine. *Balthus.* New York: The Metropolitan Museum of Art /Henry N. Abrams, Inc., 1984.

Rosenberg & Stiebel, Inc. *Sara Rossberg Figuratively Speaking.* New York, 1990.

Shaman, Sanford Sivitz. "An Interview with Philip Pearlstein." *Art in America* (September 1981):120-126.

Sims, Lowery Stokes. *The Figure in 20th Century American Art; Selections from the Metropolitan Museum of Art.* New York: The American Federation of Arts, 1984.

Stuckey, Charles F. "What's Wrong with this Picture?" *Art in America* (September 1981):96-107.

Taylor, John Russell. *Sara Rossberg, New Paintings.* London: Thumb Gallery, 1988.

Tomkins, Calvin. *Post- to Neo-: The Art World of The 1980s.* New York: Penguin Books, 1989.

In Human Terms

Paintings

MILET ANDREJEVIC

The Musician, 1978

oil on canvas

22 x 40 inches (55 x 101.6 cm)

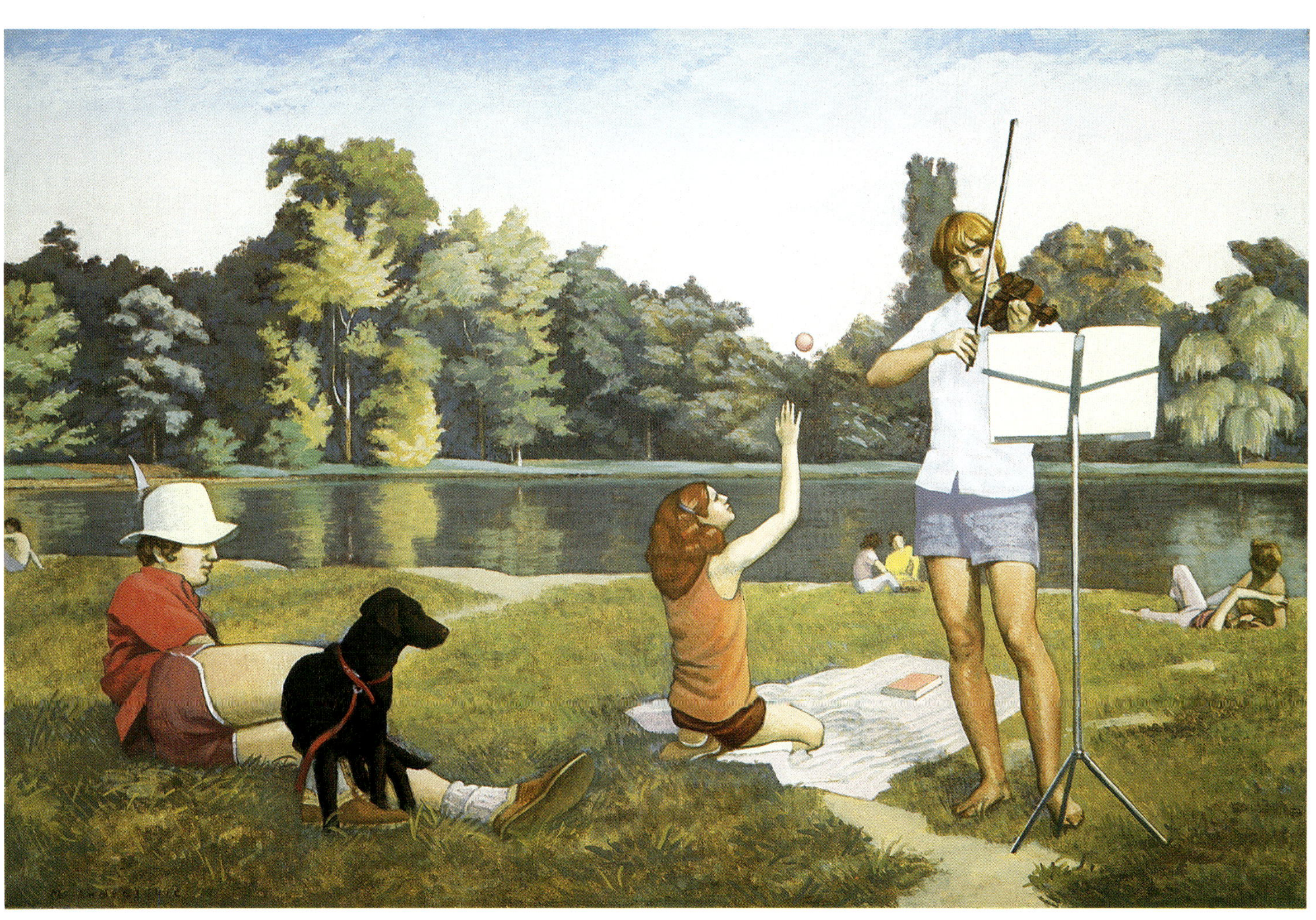

BALTHUS

Colette assise, 1954

oil on canvas

32 x 26 inches (81 x 65 cm)

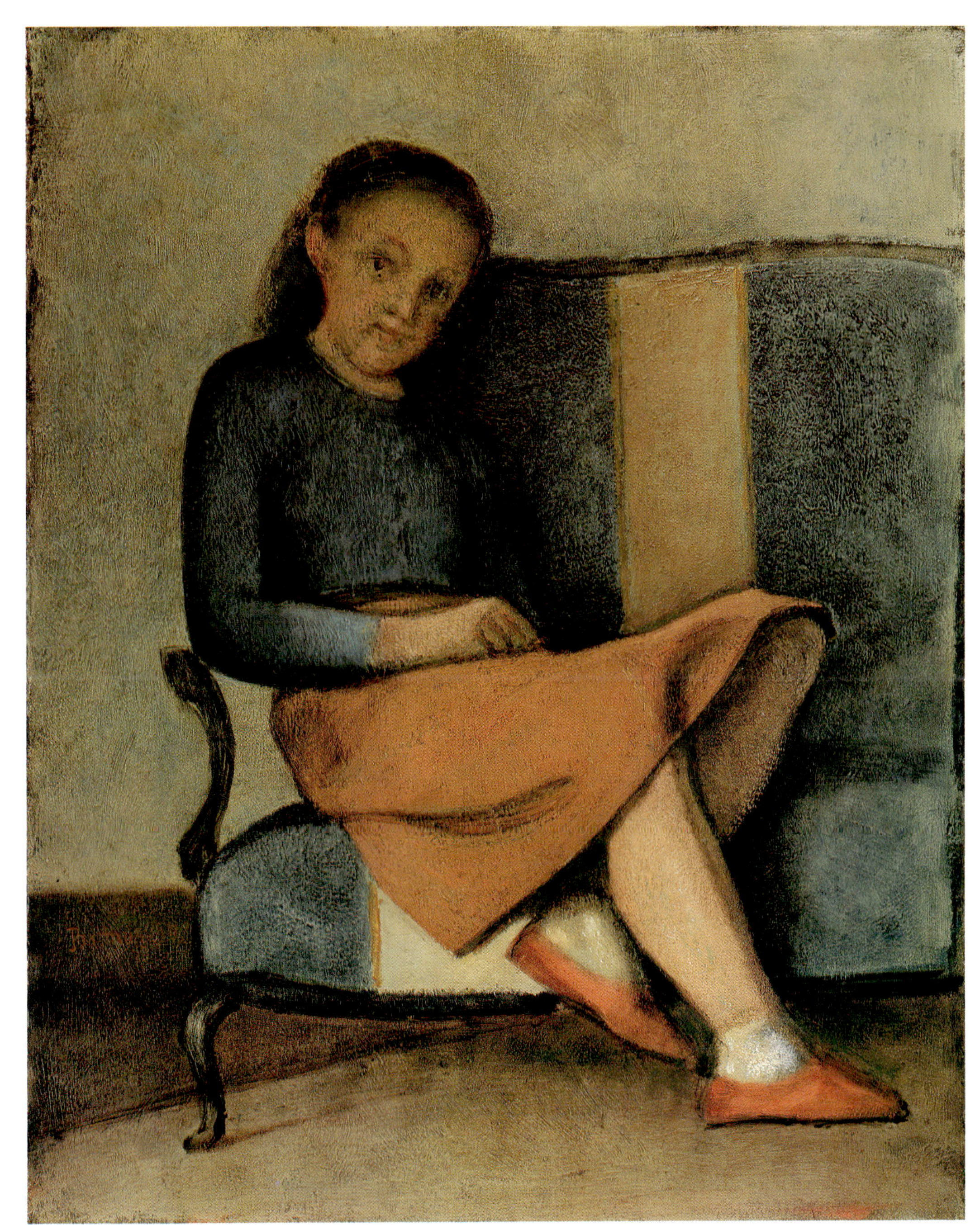

WILLIAM BECKMAN

Diana 9, 1988–90

oil on wood panel

56 x 38½ inches (142 x 97 cm)

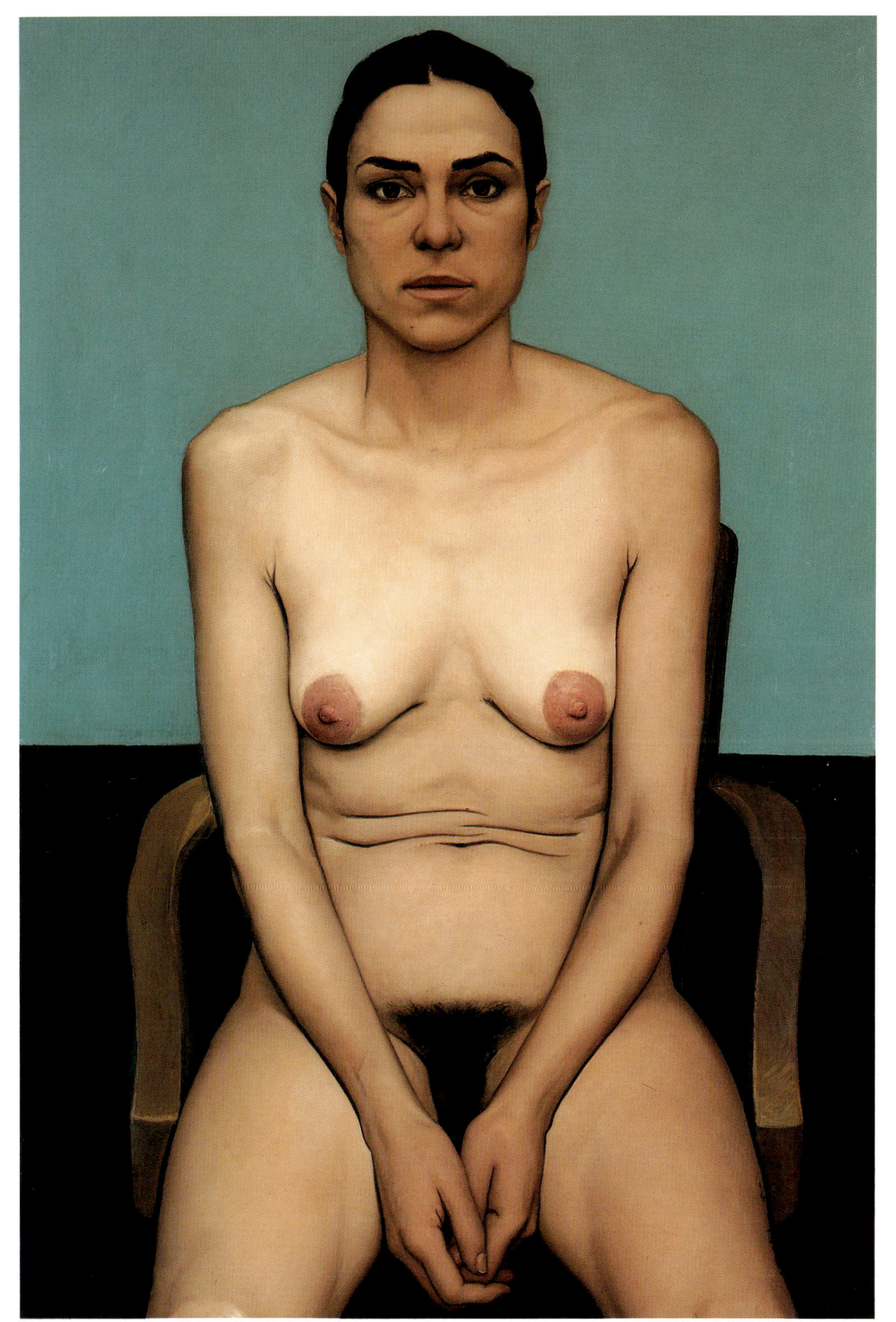

TIBOR CSERNUS

Untitled (Reclining Nude), 1980

oil on canvas

38¼ x 57½ inches (97 x 146 cm)

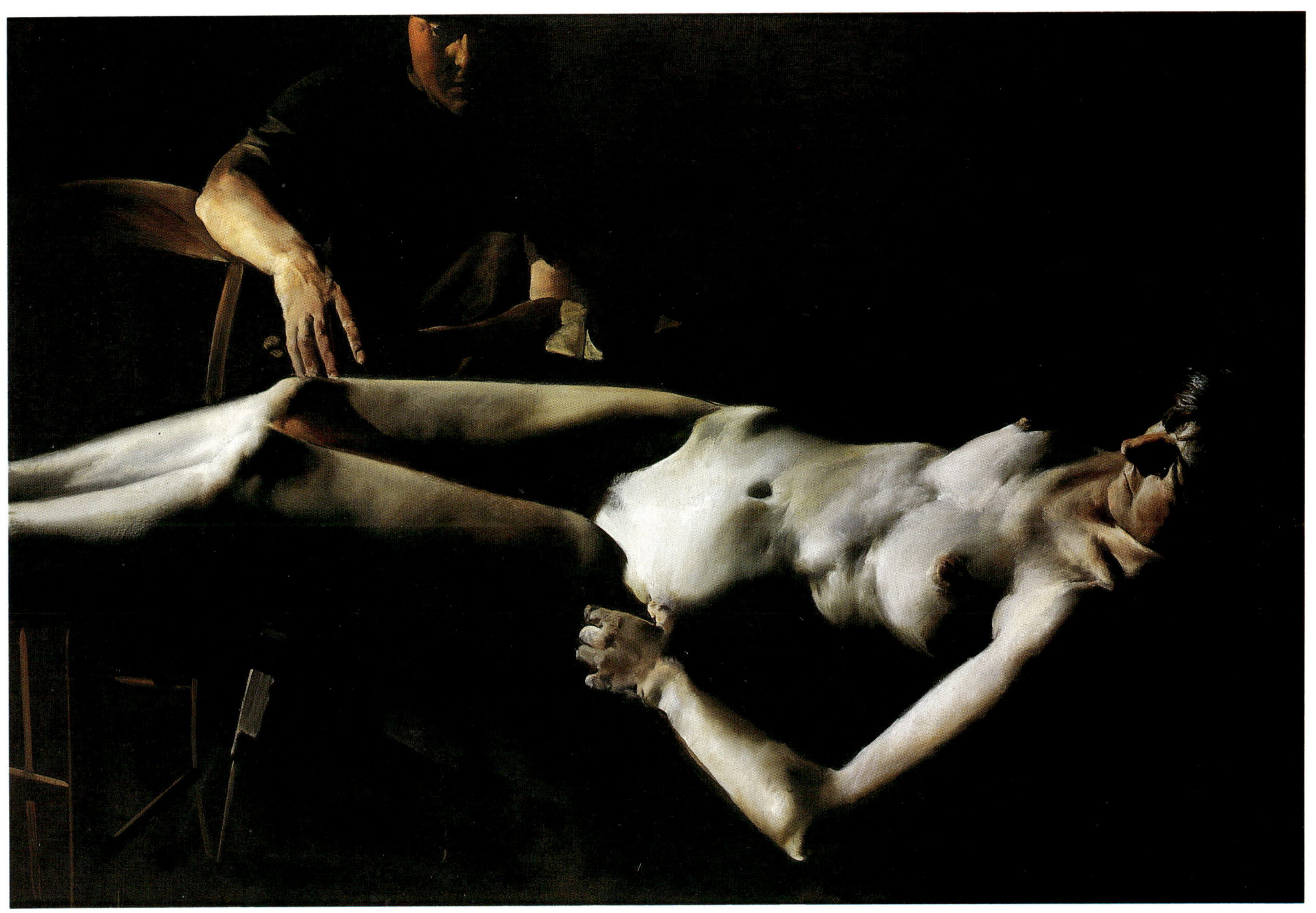

LUCIAN FREUD

Pregnant Girl, 1960–61

oil on canvas

36 x 28 inches (91.5 x 71 cm)

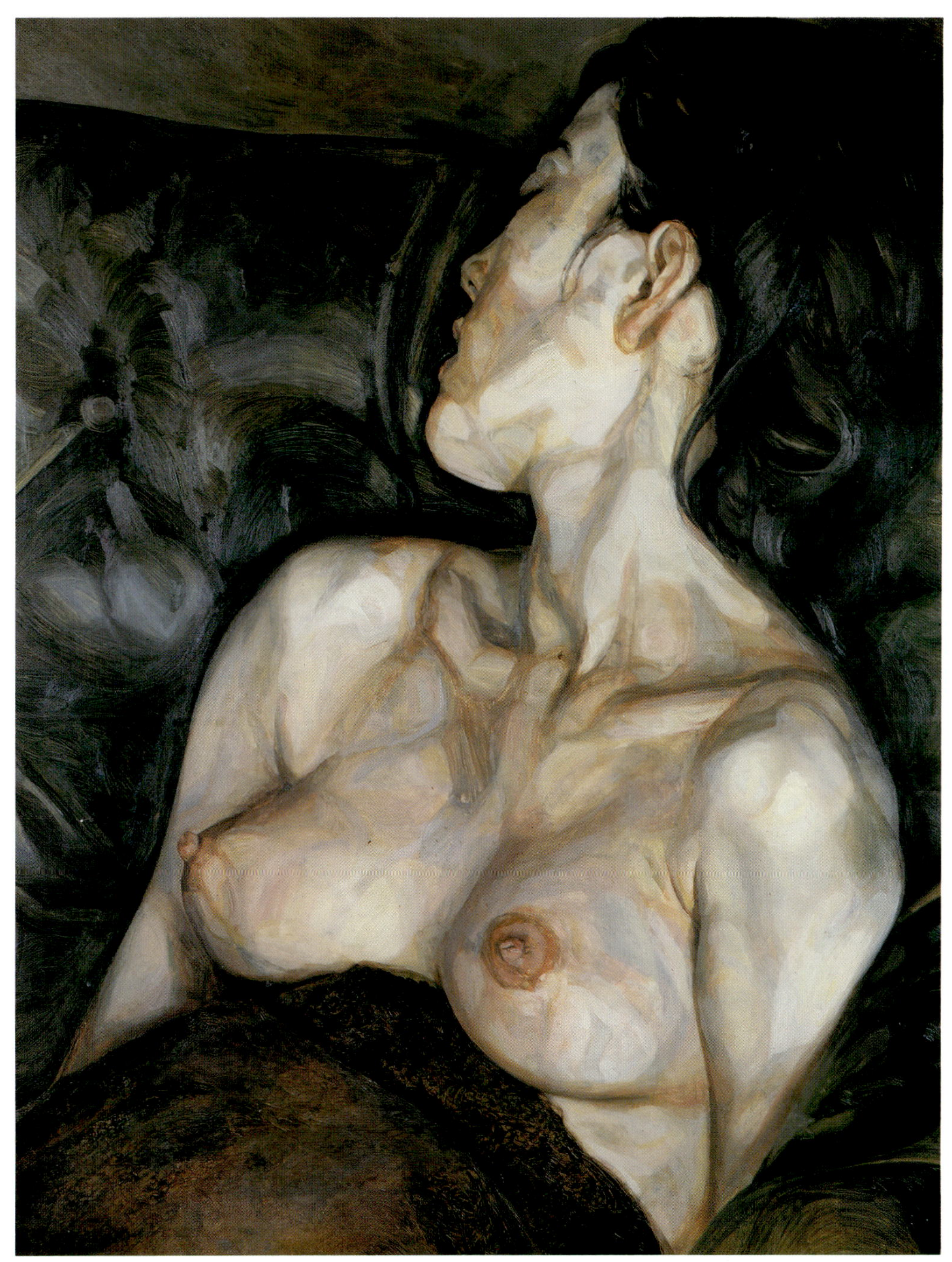

JOHN KOCH

Nude (Eating Peach), 1959

oil on canvas

20 x 18 inches (50 x 45 cm)

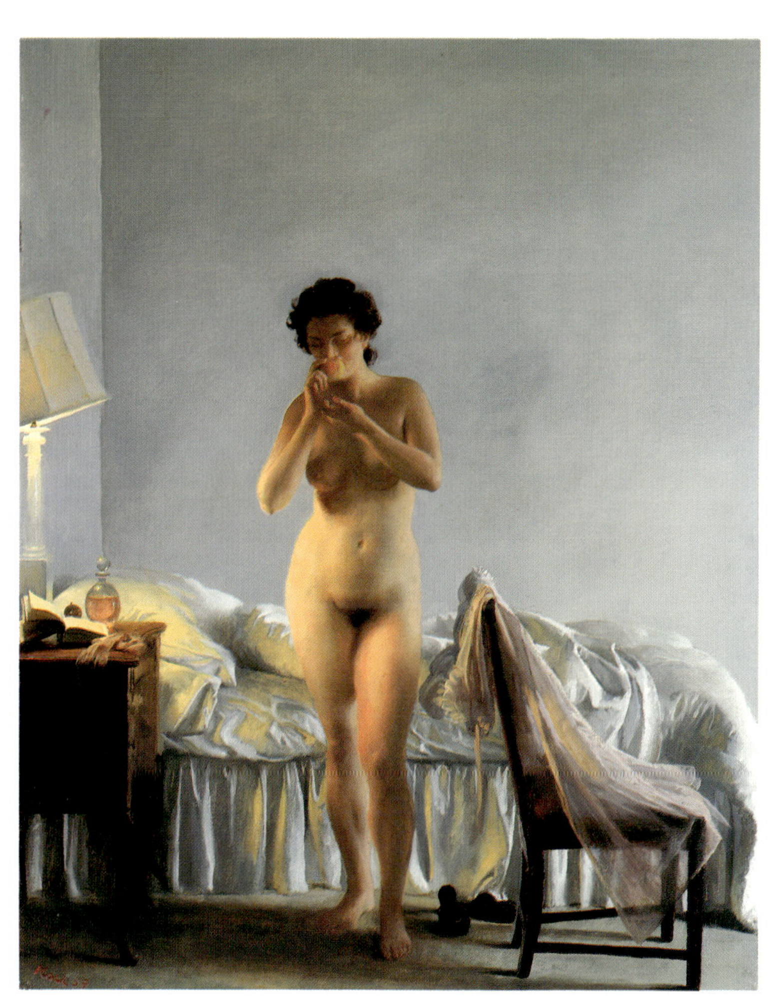

MICHAEL LEONARD

Female Bather on Gold II, 1989

oil and alkyd on masonite

26 x 27¼ inches (66 x 69 cm)

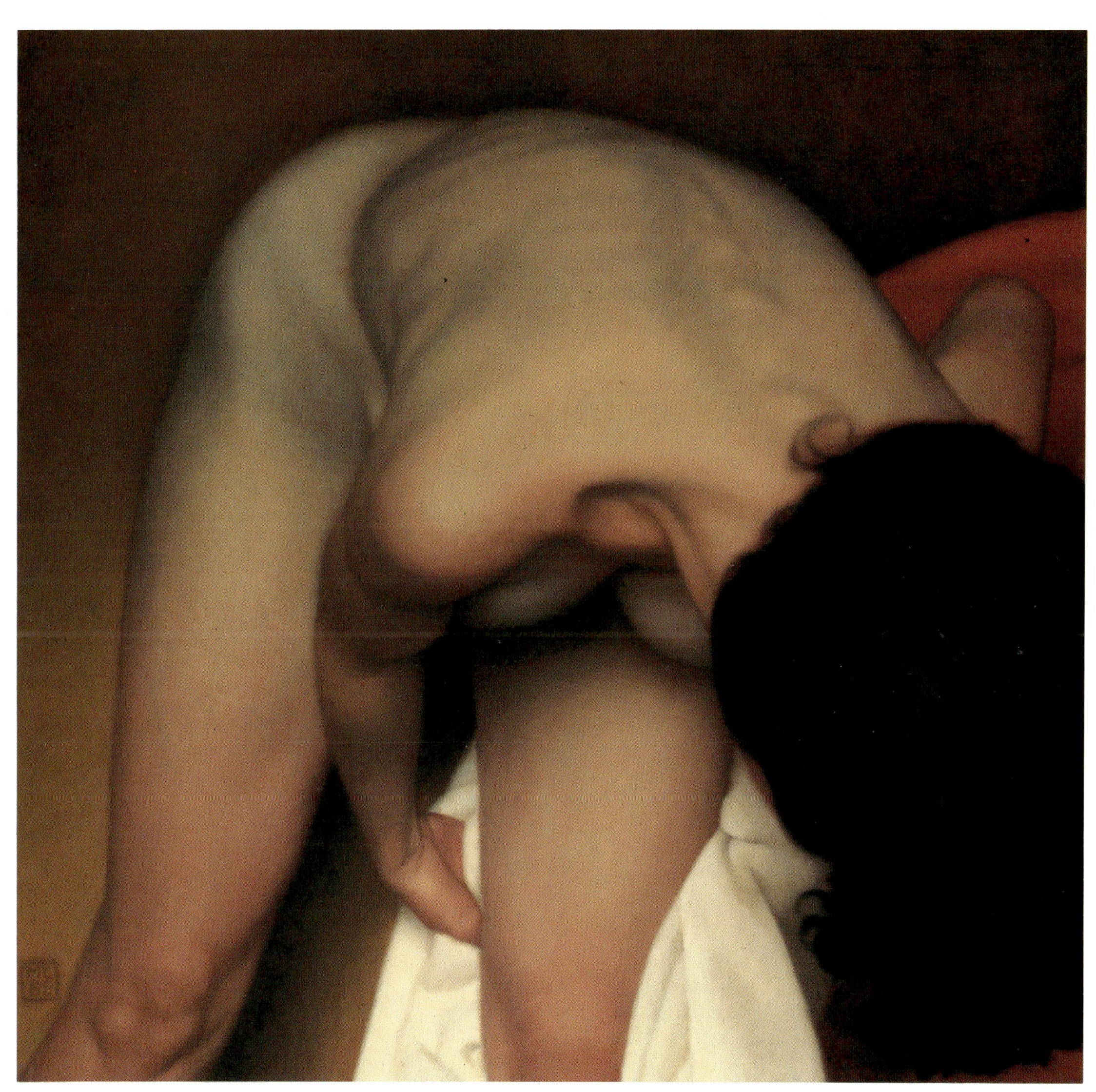

ALFRED LESLIE

Casey Key, 1983

oil on canvas

72 x 108 inches (182 x 274 cm)

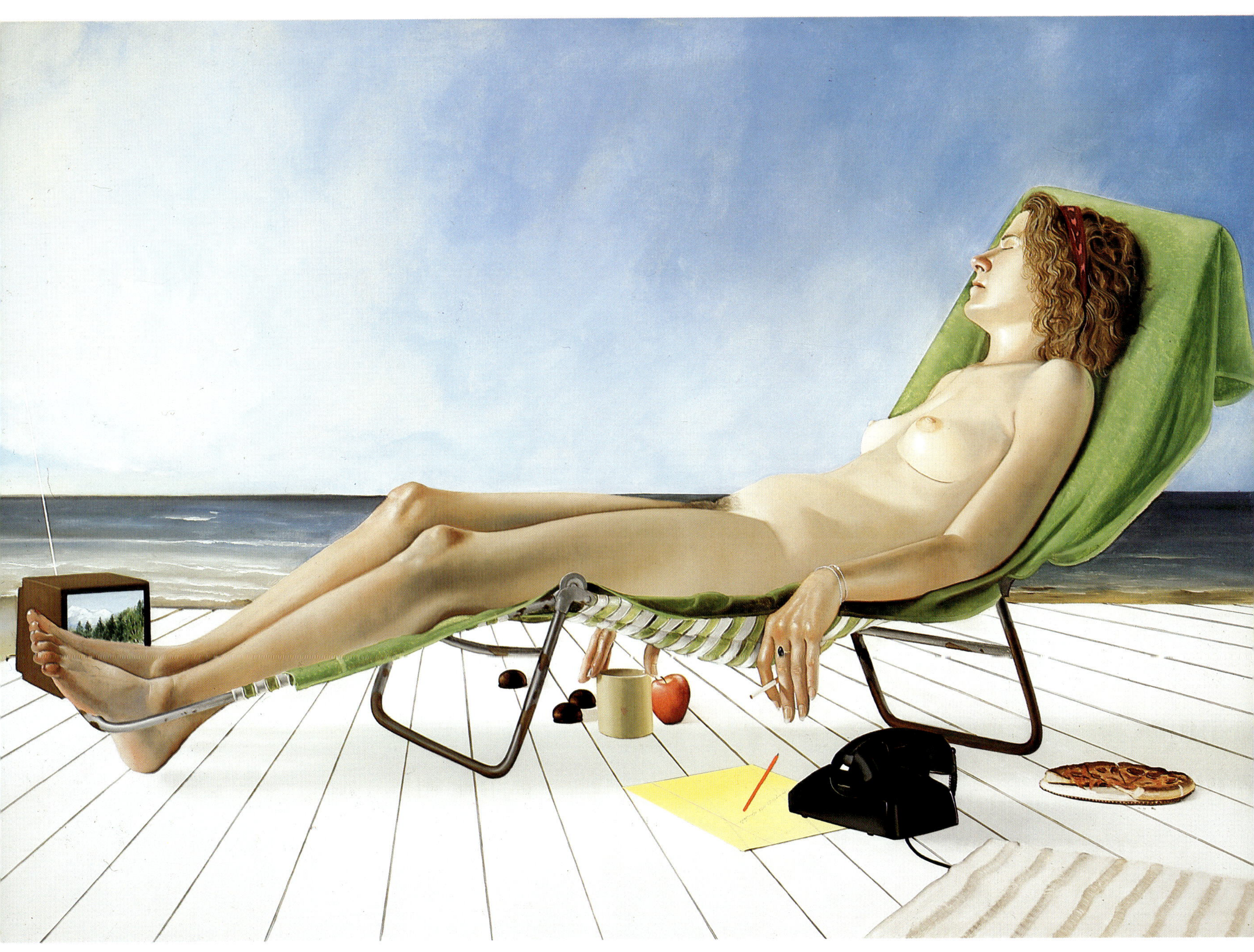

PHILIP PEARLSTEIN

Nude with Red Model Airplane, 1988

oil on linen

60 x 48 inches (152.5 x 122 cm)

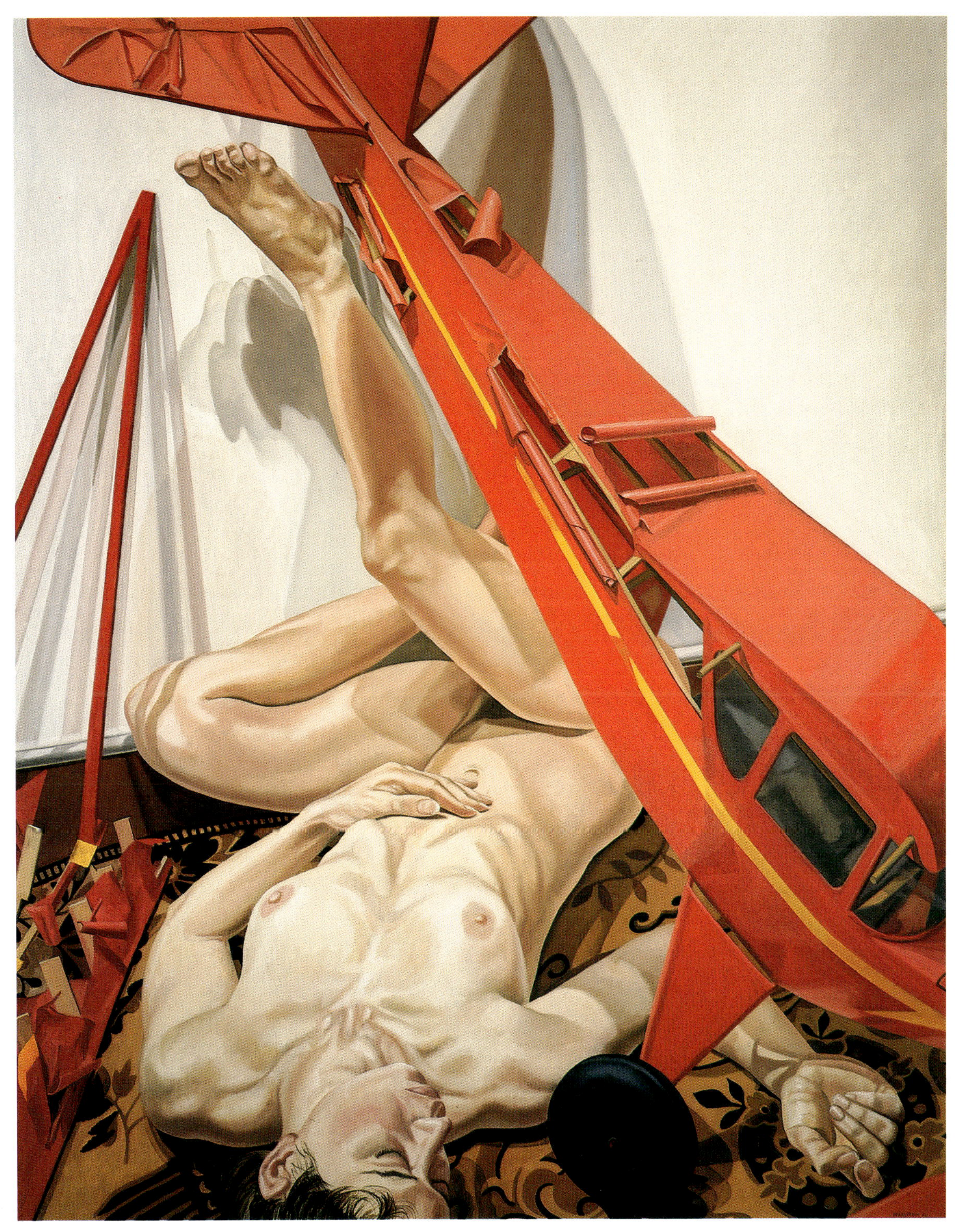

SARA ROSSBERG

Layers, 1990

acrylic on canvas

76 x 96 inches (193 x 243 cm)

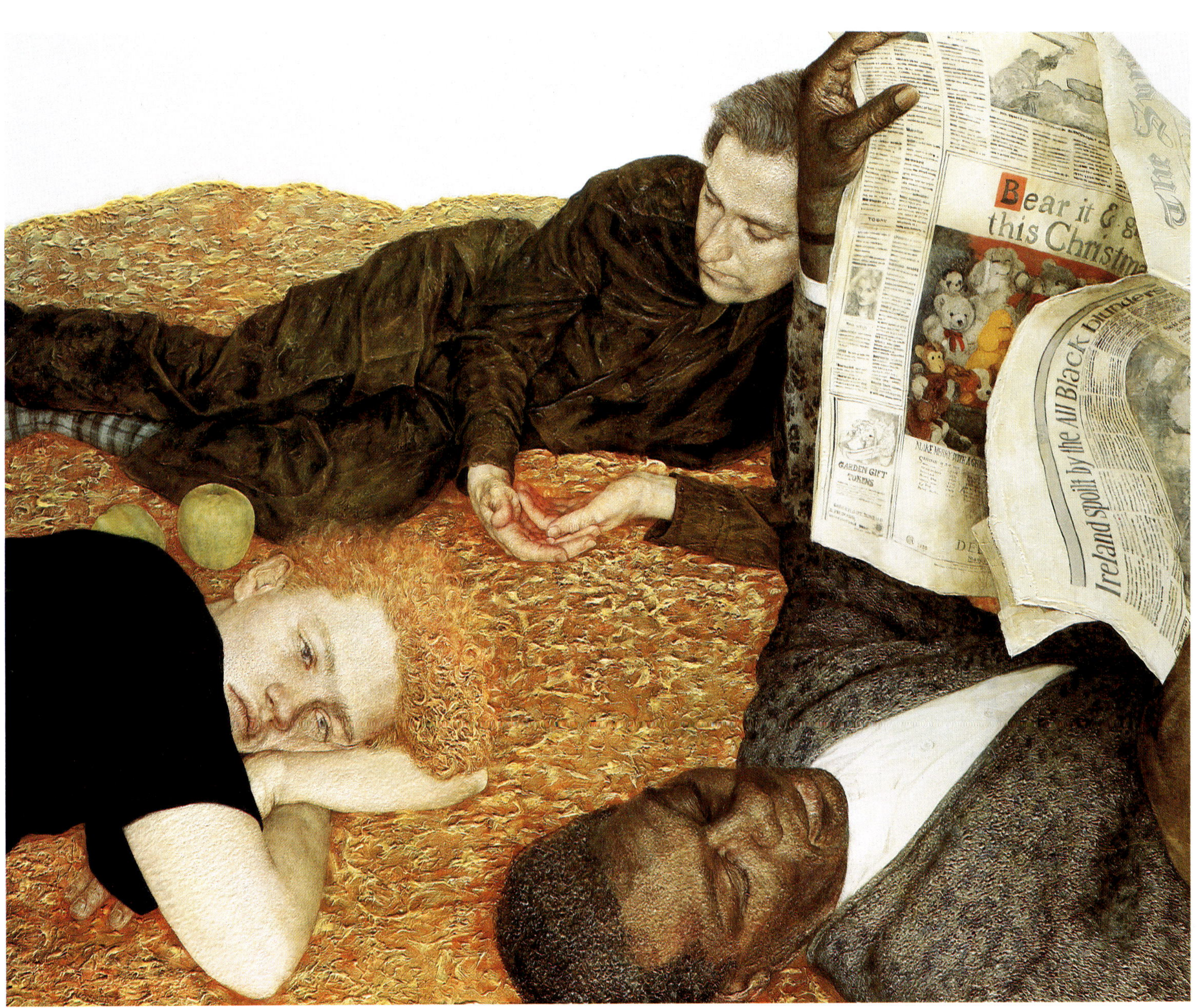

Ireland spoilt by the All Black blunders
GARDEN GIFT TOKENS

In Human Terms

Works on Paper

MILET ANDREJEVIC

Bow Bridge III, 1986

pastel and pencil on paper

10⅜ x 14½ inches (26 x 36 cm)

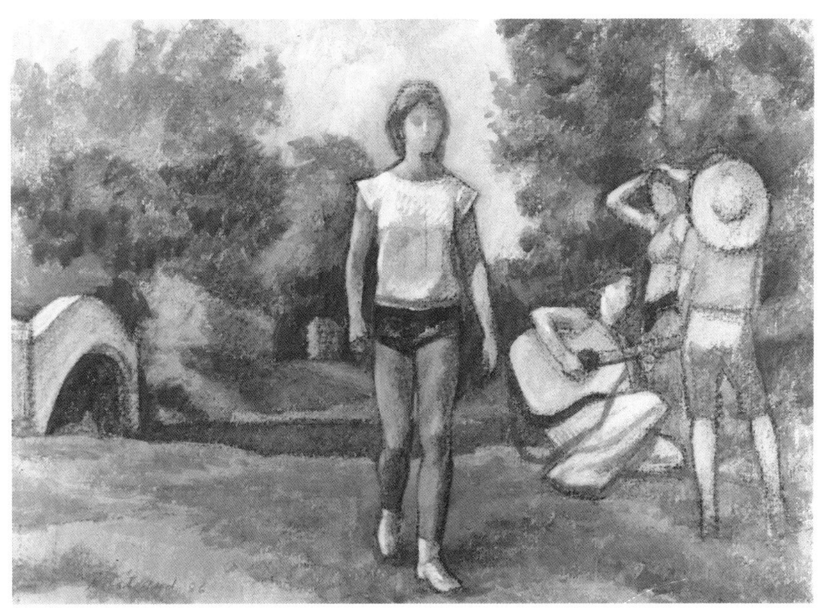

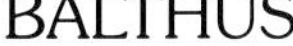

BALTHUS

Sleeping Nude, 1982

pencil on paper

13¾ x 18 inches (35 x 45 cm)

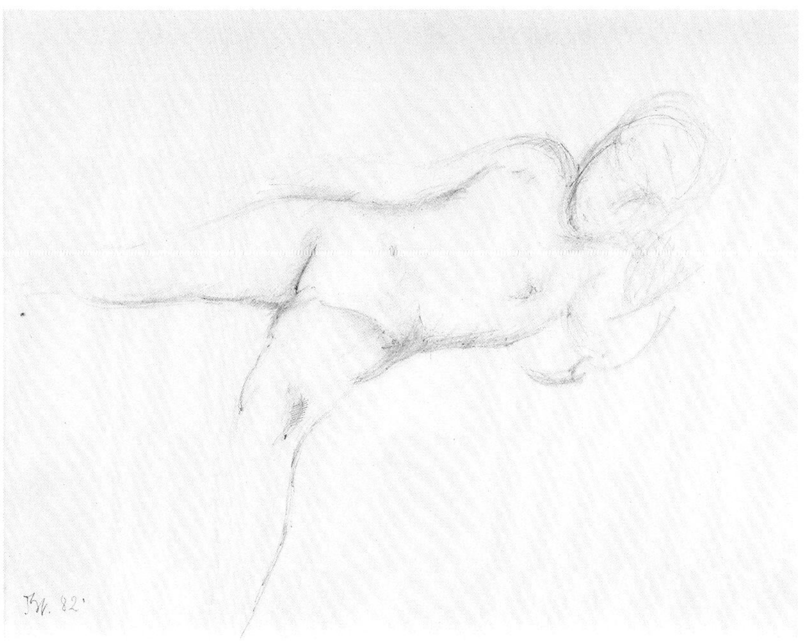

WILLIAM BECKMAN

Seated Figure #6, 1989-90

charcoal on paper

73¼ x 74 inches (186 x 187 cm)

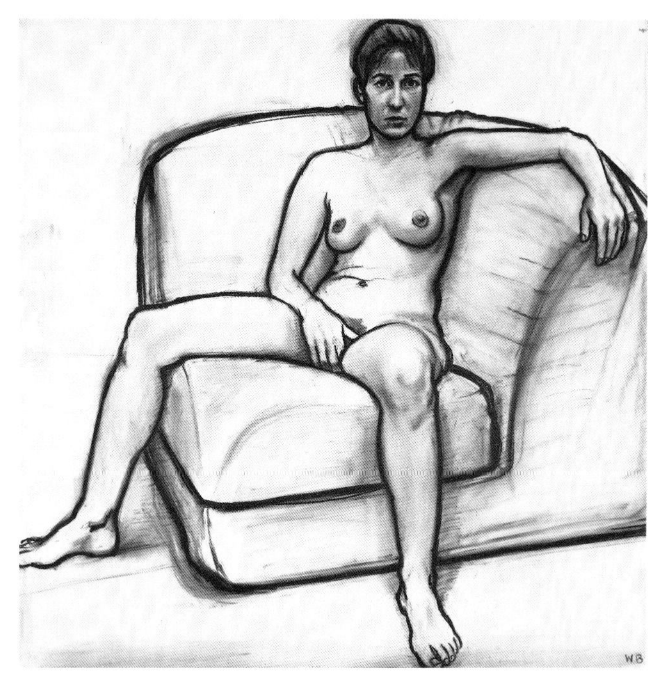

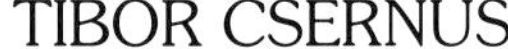

TIBOR CSERNUS

Untitled (Reclining Nude) 1989

oil pastel on paper

21 x 27 inches (55 x 70 cm)

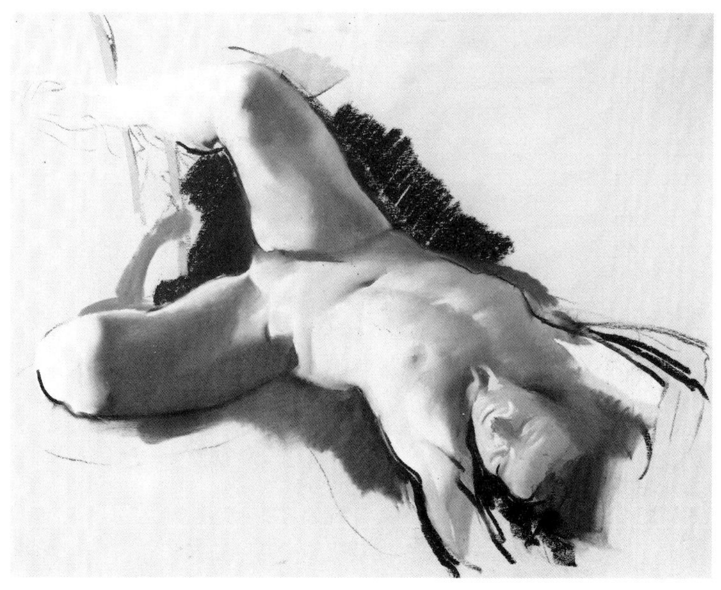

LUCIAN FREUD

Drawing After Watteau III, 1983

ink on paper

8¾ x 12⅞ inches (22 x 33 cm)

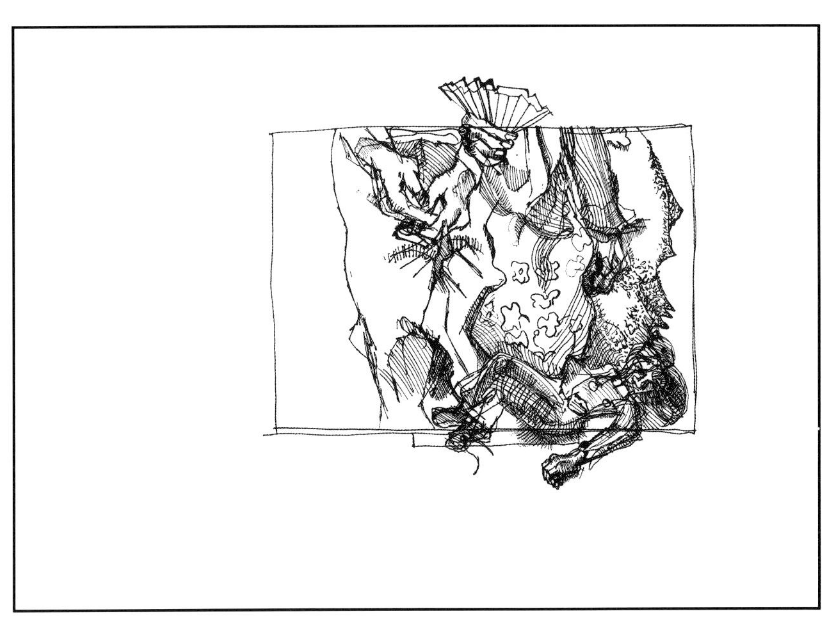

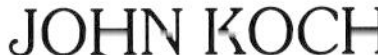

JOHN KOCH

Study for "The Monument", circa 1950

pencil and white chalk on gray paper

10 x 12¾ inches (25 x 32 cm)

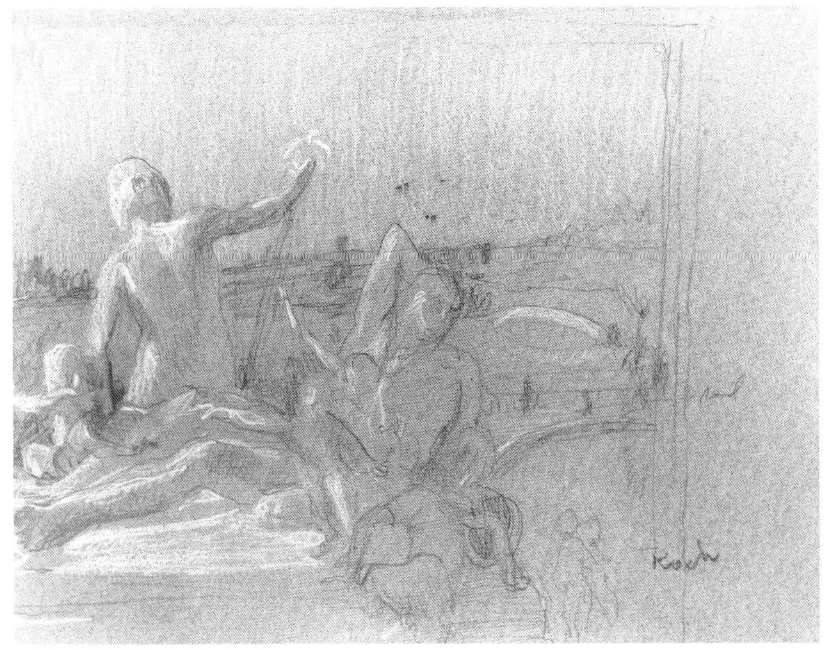

MICHAEL LEONARD

Squatting Bather, 1990

pencil on paper

8 x 8 inches (20 x 20 cm)

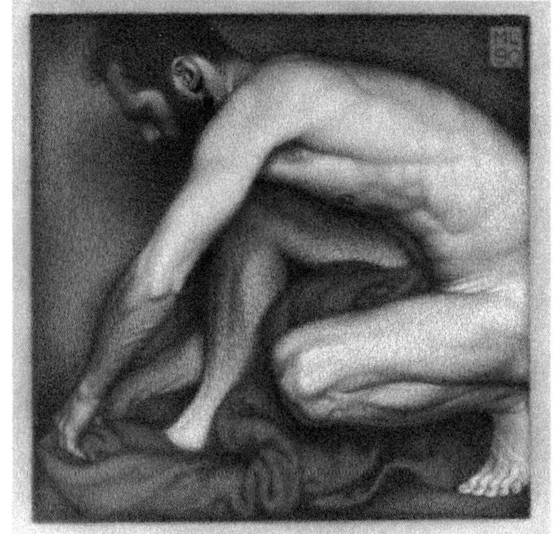

ALFRED LESLIE

The Golden Age, 1974

charcoal and pencil on paper

30 x 40 inches (76 x 101 cm)

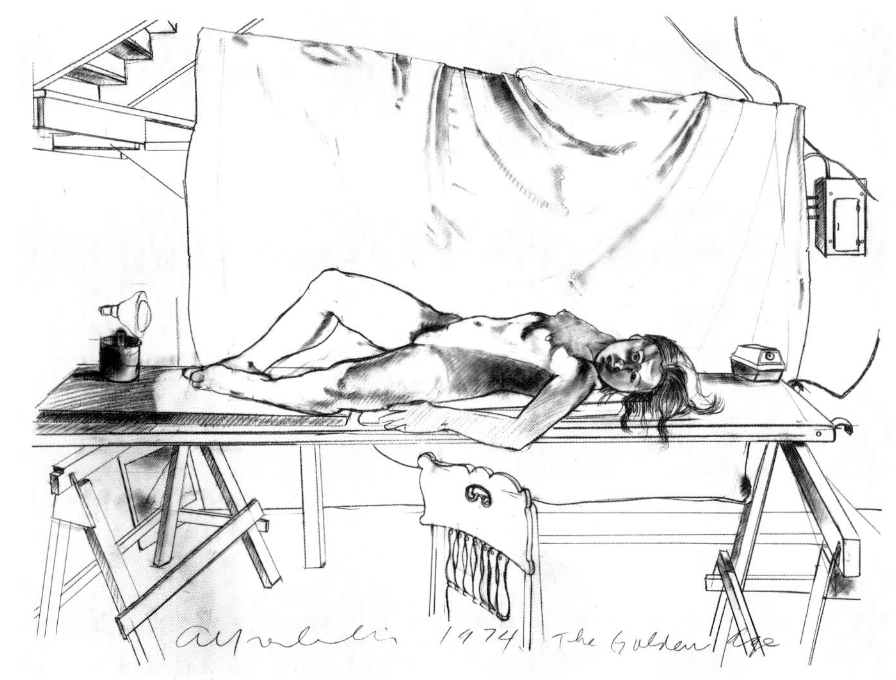

PHILIP PEARLSTEIN

Study for Nude with Horn Chair, 1989

pencil on paper

24 x 30 inches (61 x 76.2 cm)

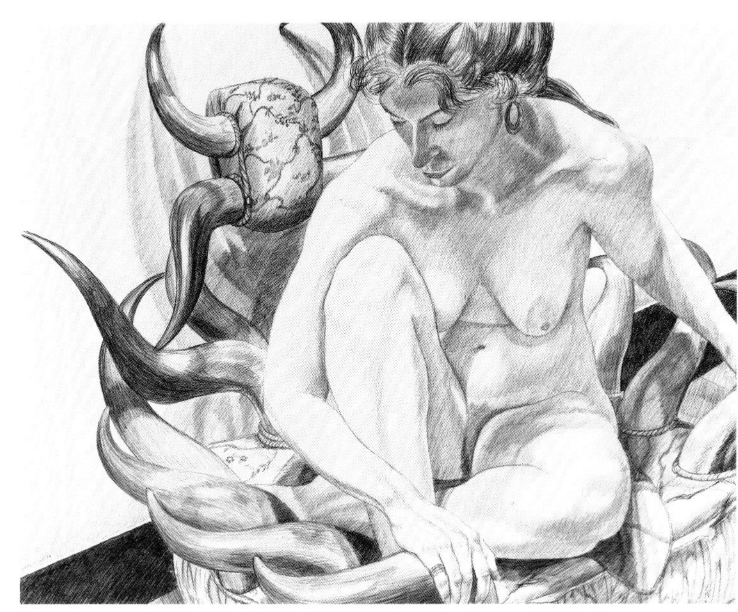

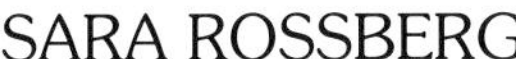

SARA ROSSBERG

One Sided, 1990

watercolor on paper

19⅝ x 15¾ inches (49.5 x 40 cm)

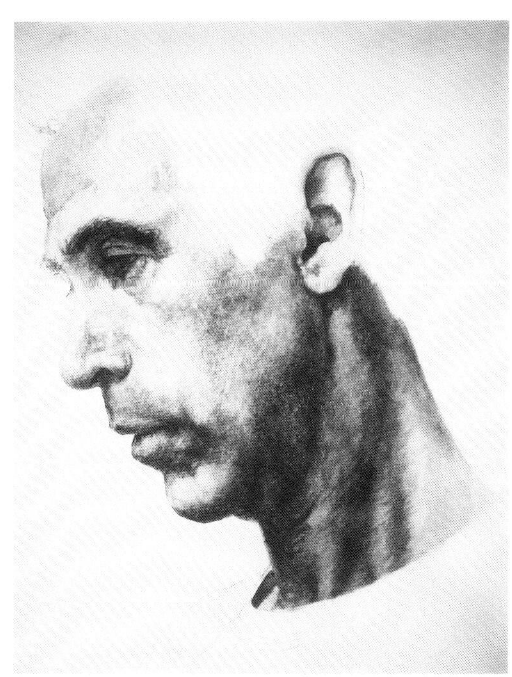

Paintings

MILET ANDREJEVIC (1925 –1989) American, born in Yugoslavia

The Musician, 1978
oil on canvas, 22 x 40 inches (55 x 101.6 cm)

Provenance: Oil & Steel Gallery, New York
Private Collection, New York

BALTHUS (Balthazar Klossowski de Rola) (born 1908) French

Colette assise, 1954
signed and dated at the back: B, 54
oil on canvas, 32 x 26 inches (81 x 65 cm)

Provenance: Skira Collection
Private Collection, New York
Galerie Jan Krugier, Geneva

Literature: *Balthus,* Centre Georges Pompidou, Musée national d'art moderne, Paris, 1983 –1984, p. 362, no. 134

Courtesy of Galerie Jan Krugier, Geneva

WILLIAM BECKMAN (born 1942) American

Diana 9, 1988 –1990
oil on wood panel, 56 x 38 1/2 inches (142 x 97 cm)

Courtesy of the artist

TIBOR CSERNUS (born 1927) Hungarian

Untitled (Reclining Nude), 1980
oil on canvas, 38¼ x 57½ inches (97 x 146 cm)

Provenance: Acquired from the artist

Exhibited: *Tibor Csernus,* Galerie Claude Bernard, Paris, 1982
Artists Choosing Artists, Artist Choice Museum, New York,1985

Literature: Jack Beal, "A Letter to Tibor Csernus," *Arts,* May 1985, pp. 130 –131
Tibor Csernus, Galerie Claude Bernard, April 1982, illustration no. 2

Courtesy of Claude Bernard Gallery, Ltd., New York

LUCIAN FREUD (born 1922) British, born in Germany

Pregnant Girl, 1960 –1961
oil on canvas, 36 x 28 inches (91.5 x 71 cm)

Provenance: John F. Parks

Exhibited: *Lucian Freud Paintings* 1947 –87, Scottish National Gallery of Modern Art, Edinburgh, 1988

Lucian Freud, Hirshhorn Museum, Washington; Hayward Gallery, London; Neue Nationalgalerie, Berlin; Centre Georges Pompidou, Musée national d'art moderne, Paris, 1987 –1988

A School of London: Six Figurative Painters, Kunstnernes Hus, Oslo; Louisiana Museum of Modern Art, Humlebaek, Denmark; Museo d'Arte Moderna Ca'Pesaro, Venice; Kunstmuseum, Düsseldorf, 1987 –1988

Lucian Freud, Arts Council of Great Britain, Hayward Gallery, 1976, no. 80 reproduced

Literature: Robert Hughes, *Lucian Freud Paintings,* London: Thames and Hudson, 1989, no. 21
Lawrence Gowing, *Lucian Freud,* London: Thames and Hudson, 1982, no. 80, reproduced p. 115

Private Collection

JOHN KOCH (1909 –1978) American

Nude (Eating Peach), 1959
Signed at lower left: Koch 59
oil on canvas, 20 x 18 inches (50 x 45 cm)

Provenance: Kraushaar Galleries
Private Collection, Michigan
Kraushaar Galleries

Courtesy of Kraushaar Galleries, New York

MICHAEL LEONARD (born 1933) British, born in India

Female Bather on Gold II, 1989
oil and alkyd on masonite, 26 x 27¼ inches (66 x 69 cm)

Courtesy of the artist

ALFRED LESLIE (born 1927) American

Casey Key, 1983
oil on canvas, 72 x 108 inches (182 x 274 cm)

Exhibited: *At the Water's Edge,* Museum of Art, Tampa; Center for the Arts, Vero Beach; Center for the Arts, Virginia Beach; The Arkansas Arts Center, Little Rock, 1989 –1991, p. 109 illustrated

Courtesy of the artist and Oil & Steel Gallery, New York

PHILIP PEARLSTEIN (born 1924) American

Nude with Red Model Airplane, 1988
signed and dated lower right: Pearlstein '88
oil on linen, 60 x 48 inches (152.5 x 122 cm)

Exhibited: *Philip Pearlstein,* Galerie Rudolf Zwirner, Cologne, 1989 (illustrated in catalogue, p. 15)

Courtesy of Hirschl & Adler Modern, New York

SARA ROSSBERG (born 1952) German

Layers, 1990
acrylic on canvas, 76 x 96 inches (193 x 243 cm)

Courtesy of Thumb Gallery, London

Works on Paper

MILET ANDREJEVIC (1925 –1989) American, born in Yugoslavia

Bow Bridge III, 1986
pastel and pencil on paper, 10⅜ x 14½ inches (26 x 36 cm)

Courtesy of Robert Schoelkopf Gallery, New York

BALTHUS (Balthazar Klossowski de Rola) (born 1908) French

Sleeping Nude, 1982
initialed and dated lower left
pencil on paper, 13 ¾ x 18 inches (35 x 45 cm)
Provenance: Thomas Ammann Fine Art, Zurich

Courtesy of James Goodman Gallery, New York

WILLIAM BECKMAN (born 1942) American

Seated Figure #6, 1989 –1990
charcoal on paper, 73 ¼ x 74 inches (186 x 187 cm)

Courtesy of the artist

TIBOR CSERNUS (born 1927) Hungarian

Untitled (Reclining Nude), 1989
oil pastel on paper, 21 x 27 inches (55 x 70 cm)

Courtesy of Galerie Claude Bernard, Paris

LUCIAN FREUD (born 1922) British, born in Germany

Drawing after Watteau III, 1983
ink on paper, 8¾ x 12⅞ inches (22 x 33 cm)

Courtesy of James Kirkman Limited, London

JOHN KOCH (1909 –1978) American

Study for "The Monument", circa 1950
signed lower right: Koch
pencil and white chalk on gray paper, 10 x 12 ¾ inches (25 x 32 cm)

Courtesy of Kraushaar Galleries, New York

MICHAEL LEONARD (born 1933) British, born in India

Squatting Bather, 1990
pencil on paper, 8 x 8 inches (20 x 20 cm)

Courtesy of the artist

ALFRED LESLIE (born 1927) American

The Golden Age, 1974
charcoal and pencil on paper, 30 x 40 inches (76 x 101 cm)

Courtesy of the artist and Oil & Steel Gallery, New York

PHILIP PEARLSTEIN (born 1924) American

Study for Nude with Horn Chair, 1989
signed and dated lower left: Pearlstein 89
pencil on paper, 24 x 30 inches (61 x 76.2 cm)

Exhibited: *Philip Pearlstein*, Galerie Rudolf Zwirner, Cologne, 1989.

Courtesy of Hirschl & Adler Modern, New York

SARA ROSSBERG (born 1952) German

One Sided, 1990
watercolor on paper, 19⅝ x 15¾ inches (49.5 x 40 cm)

Courtesy of Thumb Gallery, London

Stiebel Modern

32 East 57th Street, New York 10022 (212)759-5536

Design: H.O. Gerngross & Co., Inc.